I0190323

HOPE
as a way of life

Steve Korch

PRAISE FOR *HOPE AS A WAY OF LIFE*.

Hope as a way of life is one of those books you'll want to gift to others and keep at hand for frequent reference. (The *Practicing Hope* section at the end of each chapter is especially helpful.) Steve helps ignite a right awe of the hope we have in Christ. He promotes a fresh gratitude and excitement for the reality of it, while providing clarity regarding this often hard-to-grasp subject.
Cathy McIlvoy, Writer

Hope as a way of life is an encouraging and refreshing read. It reminds us of the correlation between our future hope in Jesus and our present activity in this life. Though it is a common theme of our faith journey, Dr. Korch helps us connect the dots in practical and inspiring ways. Each chapter felt like drinking a glass of mountain water after hiking a steep trail. It was just what I needed and I trust others will find this book does the same for them.
Louis Menjivar, Pastor

Hope is as essential to us as the air we breathe. Yet the often harsh realities of life chip away at our hope until we lose our bearings. Steve Korch's *Hope as a way of life* serves up short chapters focused on different aspects of the true source of hope as well as how to restore and maintain it in the midst of life's challenges. Honest and real, deeply true, this is a book to pick up again and again. Whether read as a personal devotional or shared with a group, this book will stir up and release strong hope, hope that sustains us through it all.

Janet Weiner, Missionary

I have been a follower of Jesus for over four decades yet I recognize my need of learning, again and again how to live in hope and ways to cultivate it. Steve Korch welcomes me into an engaging conversation where I am able to grasp hope's breadth and depth through his clear and thoughtful treatment of Holy Scripture and offers personal reflective interactions so that hope can become more and more a way of life than just an idea.

Russ Ikeda, Chaplain

to Ruthie
the girl of my dreams

HOPE as a way of life
© 2018 by Steve Korch
Published by Red Kite Publishers
Santa Cruz, California 95060
www.redkitepublishers.com

No part of this publication may be reproduced, stored in a retrieval system, or transmitted in any form or by any means, electronic, mechanical, photocopying, recording, or otherwise, without the prior permission of the copyright owner, except for brief quotations included in a review of the book.

Unless otherwise noted, Bible quotations in this volume are taken from the New American Standard Bible, © 1960, 1960, 1963, 1968, 1971, 1972, 1973, 1975, 1977, 1995 by The Lockman Foundation. Used by permission. Quotations marked (NIV) are from: HOLY BIBLE: *New International Version*, copyright © 1973, 1978, 1984. Use by permission of Zondervan Bible Publishers. Quotations marked (TLB) are from *The Living Bible*, copyright © 1971. Used by permission of Tyndale House Publishers, Inc., Wheaton, IL. 60189. All rights reserved.

Cover art & design: Holly Hawk, Holly Hawk Creative
  www.hollyhawkcreative.com

ISBN 978-0985413118 (pbk.)

Library of Congress Control Number: 2018956314
Library of Congress Subject Headings:
  Spiritual life – Christianity
  Spiritual formation
  Hope

Printed in the U.S.A.
1.1.2 (01.01.19)

GRATITUDE

Gratitude, in my mind, is more than simple thankfulness. It includes an appreciation of others and a recognition of their generosity. Gratitude sources from a place of humility that treasures the gifts others have bestowed. It is with such gratitude that I find great pleasure in acknowledging those who have brought their gifts to this project.

Although this exploration of hope has been a very personal journey, I have not traveled alone. Each thought was weighed and shaped in quiet conversations with my closest friend and deepest love in this world ... my wife. This book would never have been written without Ruthie. It is as much hers as it is mine.

I am grateful for those who were willing to invest in the project as readers. Three of those who made significant contributions to the manuscript were Jessica Hoff, Cathy McIlvoy and Becky Kimball. Becky's comments and insights were particularly significant and I've incorporated much of what she offered into the book ... with her permission.

In the production of this book, I am grateful for Noel Smith's editing and for the original cover art produced by my daughter, Holly Hawk.

I treasure the generous gifts from those who have invested in this project.

CONTENTS

introduction

An Overwhelming Hope

"I know the plans I have for you,"
declares the Lord, …
plans to give you **hope**." Jeremiah 29:11

I didn't set out to write a book on hope. In fact, I launched into this project because the concept of hope seemed a bit fuzzy to me. It was an under-developed idea in my thinking—a word without a clear definition. Hope seemed to be a term that was used to convey uncertainty about the future, sort of a fingers-crossed, wishful thinking attitude. However, there were two realities that squirreled around in my mind. The first was the rather universal assertion that hope is a vital element for survival on planet earth. Hope is what keeps us moving forward in both the good times and the hard times. If we lose hope, we have no reason to continue on.

The other reality brought an additional

layer of intrigue to my perception of hope. I found that hope is to be one of the distinguishing marks of anyone who claims to have found new life in Jesus. Hope is presented in the Bible as an observable quality that shapes every aspect of life. Hope is characterized as more than an asset to life; it is cast as a life-altering perspective—a way life.

So I decided to make hope the focus of my personal research for the space of a year. With the Bible as my primary database, I began blogging my discoveries and inviting others into the conversation. Along the way, the project became a journey and took on a life of its own. My understanding of hope was challenged by encounters with individuals who were searching for a hope bigger than themselves, one that would carry them through life as they were experiencing it. These included a young husband trying to imagine life after the death of his wife, a single woman struggling with loneliness, and a father facing his addiction. There were many other stories. Some sounded more commonplace, but not to those who owned them. Although my hope blogs lasted only a few months, the journey has continued for years. The pages that follow are my attempt to share what I've discovered about hope.

Now, I realize there are thousands of books on hope already in print. Many of them present helpful insights and offer practical assistance to those in need of hope. Many of them are filled with inspiring stories and personal accounts of those who have found hope in every conceivable circumstance. There are books written by counselors and therapists, pastors and theologians, celebrities and experts. It would seem that the subject of hope has been exhausted. So how is this book different?

First of all, this book is about hope *as a way of life*. It is a hope so compelling that it recasts our identity, redefines life and reshapes what matters most. It is a hope so powerful that it alters how we orient ourselves in a broken world. We will be considering a hope that has the ability to capture our heart, invade all our thoughts and exceed our wildest imagination. It is a hope that is too good to be true, and yet it is authentic.

Secondly, this book is about a hope *that transforms how we experience the realities of life*. It's a hope that changes how we face both the pleasures and challenges that are common to all of us. We will explore a hope that has the potential to deepen our enjoyment of the best this life has to offer and to carry us through the worst this life can throw at us.

Does such hope truly exist? It does.

Is it possible to experience such hope? It is.

Where do we look to find this hope? Good question!

You won't find it in the self-help section of your bookstore or in the bestseller section on Amazon. Instead, it's found in a place you may have discarded as seemingly irrelevant and out-of-date ... the Bible. I'm convinced that's the only place where any real words of hope can be found.

This book is designed with smaller dimensions in order to make it more inviting. It has been written with short chapters, more like brief meditations. I believe that the ideas considered in this book are better absorbed in small doses, a little at a time.

In the following chapters, we will engage in fifteen brief conversations about hope. I don't intend to offer any shallow slogans or simplistic advice, no spiritual antidepressants. You won't find "5 easy steps" for becoming a more hopeful person. Instead, what you *will* find is an honest attempt to help us encounter some of the most encouraging truth that could ever be found.

I consider it an honor and a privilege to have these conversations with you, the reader. I have undertaken this endeavor with great care and concern. I've imagined us sitting together face-to-face and talking about life, the good and the bad, the pleasant and the painful. I've tried to anticipate some of the questions we might raise and how we might talk through them. I've lived long enough to know that there is not an answer for every question, but that there *are* insights that help move the conversation along. I know that your circumstances in life are unique to you and yet common to all of us. But whatever those circumstances are, I would like you to come away from each conversation encouraged.

There is hope!

1

Fingers Crossed

"For we do not want you to be unaware, brethren, of our affliction which came to us in Asia, that we were burdened excessively beyond our strength, so that we despaired even of life; indeed, we had the sentence of death within ourselves in order that we should not trust in ourselves, but in God who raises the dead; who delivered us from so great a peril of death, and will deliver us, He on whom we have set our **hope**." Corinthians 1:8-10

I think our world's hope reserves are running pretty close to empty ... at least in our culture. We are wrestling with huge questions, all of us—the same questions the major religions all try to address. Can we expect good, or not? Is everything ever going to be okay? Is there a reason for my pain? Our world's pain? Is there a higher purpose in all this? So many genuine, agonizing questions. The fact that you are reading this book probably says something about you and about what's happening in your life right now. Your own hope reserves may be just about tapped out. These questions may be very personal and more practical than philosophical.

We all need hope. Like when our present circumstances look bleak or when life doesn't seem to make any sense; when we fear some possibility in the future—near or far; when we have invested ourselves in some future possibility; when there is something we really want, but don't yet have.

Chances are, all of us have our hopes tied to at least one of these scenarios at any given moment. Perhaps, if we sat together over dinner and a glass of wine, we might venture into one of our stories of hope filled with personal details and vivid animation. Speaking of our hopes and fears takes us into the deepest part of who we are. Such conversations, if they are honest, reveal what shapes our lives and explains our actions.

The Apostle Paul reveals some of his deepest thoughts in a missionary letter sent to one of his supporting churches. Even as one of the stalwart leaders in the early church and a courageous man of faith, Paul found himself breathing only thin vapors of hope. His honesty is poured out in this confession:

"we were burdened excessively beyond our strength, so that we despaired even of life"

These words express an experience common to all of us. Serving as a pastor for more than twenty years, I often found myself sitting with those whose lives had just fallen apart and were searching for some shred of hope to cling to. Their stories covered the full range of human experience—death of a child, discovery of cancer, loss of a job, divorce, financial ruin, natural disasters. They were *"burdened excessively beyond their strength."* I would listen as they attempted to put words to their experience and describe the emotions that dominated the present. Although every story was unique and personal, there were common threads that ran through all of them. You probably fill them in from your own experiences.

I too know first-hand what those dark valleys look like and feel like. I have my own stories of crisis and of life seeming to fall apart. Revisiting those memories, I believe that some of the common threads I heard from others could also have been heard from me.

One such experience remains a graphic image in my memory as I walked through a very personal and public crisis that appeared suddenly and unexpectedly (like most crises do). I can vividly recall feeling sick to my stomach, disoriented and wondering if all was lost. I felt lethargic, drained of energy. I found myself fearful of what might lie ahead. That fear was amplified at night when my dreams had the freedom to conjure up the worst possible scenarios. I found it difficult to think beyond the present, yet pressed by a sense of urgency.

Sound familiar?

We all have some measure of hope. We can't survive without it. And yet the uncertainty of our hope may cause us to hedge our bets. There's an old English proverb from the 1800s that has endured until today: *"Hope for the best, but plan for the worst."* It's a common philosophy for life that longs for something positive in the future, fingers crossed, but operates under the assumption that the realities of life are more likely. Such hope seems rather thin, more like a mental coping device to keep ourselves from drowning in life as it presents itself.

When life is rough with us, we search for any source of hope, anything that can help us make it through, a life preserver for the soul to keep us from drowning in the churning seas of life. When our hope reserves run low, the vitality of life drains away. The psalmist put it this way: *"Hope deferred makes the heart grow sick."* (Proverbs 13:12). He captures what we experience when what we have counted on hasn't materialized; when life as we have imagined it doesn't match our expectations. Hope deferred is like a mirage that keeps moving out of reach. Paul sounds heartsick when he writes,

"we despaired even of life"

As we face the uncertainties of life, the real issue is not one of hoping more intently, but of considering the source of our hope. We all have hope in something. This begs the question of hope in what. No one wants to feel the fool. We want hope rooted in truth ... something more than a fingers-crossed hope. Deep down we sense that hope sourcing from ourselves isn't big or strong enough, and that hope sourcing from others is too fragile. We're left still searching.

Paul's experience of affliction, burden and despair forced him to consider the source of his hope. He concluded that any hope of his own making was not enough and that he must set his hope on something, rather on some*one*, who was willing and capable to secure his future.

"He on whom we have set our hope."

PURSUING HOPE

- When have you felt you were losing hope? What caused that loss of hope?

- How would you describe your experience?

- Does that old English proverb *"Hope for the best, but plan for the worst"* describe how you approach hope? Why?

PRACTICING HOPE

- Make a list of questions you have concerning hope.

- Begin a habit of inviting God into your hope questions.

- Invite someone to be a companion with you as you read this book.

PERSONAL NOTES

fingers crossed

2

THE ECONOMICS OF HOPE

"In You, O LORD, I have taken refuge;
Let me never be ashamed. …
For You are my hope:
O LORD God, You are my confidence."
Psalm 71:1 & 5

I 've heard it said that two of life's best gifts
are memory and hope. One connects us to
the past and the other to the future. Memory
allows us to collect our past experiences and
piece together our personal story as it has
played out to the present. For most of us, it
usually includes a hodgepodge assortment of
mismatched images and short clips from
random events. Memory allows us to revisit
pleasant times and inhale the fragrance of
those moments. We can gaze into the eyes of
a loved one and recall experiences that have
shaped who we have become. Memory also
preserves fragments of wisdom, often

attaching them to a specific episode of our story. Memory is indeed a gift.

While memory offers the possibility of revisiting our past, hope attempts to envision our future. Our history has been written and the storyline has led us to the present. But the story's not over. Even as you read these words your story is moving forward. Hope is a word that captures how we picture what may lie ahead, envisioning the best possible scenarios. Hope battles its archenemy, fear, for the power to shape how we face whatever is next for us.

Life could be described as a continuous story of hope—optimistic dreams for the future, expectations for something better, confidence in favorable outcomes. It enters much of life as we cling to the possibility that somewhere in the future there may be some kind of rescue or redemption or reconciliation, perhaps the healing of a relationship or of a disease, maybe the escape from a nightmare. Hope seems to stamp every aspect of our story. It determines how we move through life by shaping how we imagine what lies ahead.

As hope enters any story, it adds a sense that no matter what the current circumstances are, things will turn out better in the end. It's like oxygen for the soul. It seems that every part of our story needs to have an underlying subplot of hope that fills its lungs and keeps the story progressing. I believe that much of life is spent searching for a hope substantial enough to keep us moving forward, a counterbalance to the fear and uncertainty that smugly leers at us from just beyond the present.

Neuroscientists tell us that we are hardwired to be optimists—to be hopeful.[1] That natural tendency toward hope is fueled by possibilities (realistic or not) and/or promises (valid or not). Hope is what comes from imagining a future based upon those possibilities or promises. It's a confident expectation that the future, as we envision it, may actually happen. Hope plays a powerful role in our lives. It can ease the weight of life or stir the soul with excitement. Hope can be the source of needed courage or the basis for

---

[1] Tali Sharot offered a concise explanation of this in a TEDTalk, February 2012.
https://www.ted.com/talks/tali_sharot_the_optimism_bias

eager anticipation. And in the space between those, hope can be what settles the soul with a quiet rest in what lies ahead, a sense of well being that allows our fragile spirit to relax.

For many, hope is a vague concept with a somewhat blurred meaning. That's understandable since it seems to be used as a synonym for faith, at times indistinguishable and therefore lost in the vocabulary of those who follow Jesus. Words like faith and believe sound more confident, more like we're trusting God's statements and counting them as true. By comparison, hope may sound less certain, maybe even timid or unsure.

Perhaps a way to think of hope is as psychological/emotional currency. We all hope in something, whether we realize it or not. We carry hope in our pockets and spend it on different things—on ideas about who we'll marry, or our kids, or leaving a meaningful legacy, achieving a sense of well-being, or on God, on forever, on Christ being in us and using us in our world, on there being something/someone else at work here beyond what meets the eye.

We all have some amount of hope. We need it to survive. Some of us have felt close to that utterly decimating, hopeless state. (remember: hope deferred makes the heart sick) But we still have some trace of hope within us—that glimmer of gold (may be fools gold, maybe not) and we're putting it somewhere. Spending it. Investing it. Banking on it. The question is what the exchange rate is on the particular hope currency we carry. And whether the source/focus of our hope is good for anything. Whether the investment is wise. What happens when we go to cash it in.

So when David says, "*You are my hope, O LORD,*" he's spending his currency on what he knows to be true and on the One who guarantees his account. In Psalm 25:3 he writes, *"No one whose hope is in you will ever be put to shame."* No bounced checks.

As believers in Jesus, our hope is in something utterly secure. The uncertainty implied by "hope" isn't about the hoping itself but about the essence of what our hope is in. If we spend our emotional/psychological currency on what is secure, then we know our hope is secure. Our currency is good. If we spend it on what may or may not turn out well, our hope becomes an optimistic wish for a positive outcome. Fingers crossed. The market is weaker, our hope less secure.

The focus of our hope, the account that our hope-checks are written against is what makes all the difference. It's not a matter of somehow hoping differently, or hoping better or using the word in a different way. True hope is only true because the focus of it is absolutely infallible.

PURSUING HOPE

- What possibilities and/or promises are fueling your sense of hope?

- Where are you spending your hope currency?

- What are you counting on to be true in the future in order to feel confident in the present?

PRACTICING HOPE

- Read Psalm 131, and then paraphrase it in your own words.

- Begin a "Hope" journal to track your journey in search of hope.

- Pray, asking Him to help you experience the hope He offers.

PERSONAL NOTES

the economics of hope

3

LOOKING BEYOND OURSELVES

"Blessed is the one whose hope is in the LORD and whose hope is the LORD." Jeremiah 17:7

In the final years of the 7th century BC, the prophet Jeremiah spoke to his society about how they had overvalued themselves and placed their hopes in their own genius instead of in Yahweh. Their focus had turned inward and they had become the heroes of their own stories. The prophet forecast the inevitable failure of such thinking, but also presented the good news of an alternative.

"Blessed is the one whose hope is in the LORD and whose hope is the LORD."

Read Jeremiah's words again … slowly. This one verse closes in on a source of hope that is utterly secure, one that offers freedom from our brokenness and promise for our deepest desires, a source of hope that never fails. Therefore, it would be worth our effort to examine this layered statement in more detail.

First of all, notice that these words speak of a hope that looks outside of us. The focus is on the LORD—Yahweh[2]—the God of our redemption. It is not a hope that is counting on philosophy, methodology or scheming. It's not wishful thinking that all will turn out well. Rather, it is confidence in a specific Someone who has made explicit promises and has the ability to deliver them. It is hope *in* Yahweh.

I believe this means that in order to activate such hope, we must continually acknowledge that we are not enough for the common demands of this life and certainly not enough for the greater challenges that we encounter along the way. It means that we must repeatedly give up the desperate attempt to be the hero of our own story and willingly give that role to the one who is our Redeemer God. We must choose to place full confidence in Him as our only true hope.

---

[2] *Yahweh* is God's personal name. See Exodus 3:14

Jeremiah then goes further and addresses the object of the hope. He identifies both the means and the end. It's not only a hope in the LORD as the hero of the story; a means to something we desire. He is also the *fulfillment* of such a hope. He is Himself the great reward—the longing of the soul. This is the game-changer!

It's one thing for us to realize that we are inadequate and to seek help from the LORD, but that's only half of the equation presented in this ancient text. God does not offer Himself as the enabler of our misdirected dreams. He offers *Himself* as the *fulfillment* of those dreams. The assertion only works as a whole, not in part.

The outcome of such hope is captured in one word: *blessed*. The prophet presents this outcome in stark contrast to all other formulas for hope. Back up two verses and we read, *"Doomed to disappointment and failure is the one who risks everything by placing hope in the earthly things of this life and counting on oneself to be enough for whatever lies ahead."*

Jeremiah announces that anyone who centers their hope in the LORD discovers a dramatically different outcome. "Blessed" is a word that expresses a sense of being favored or fortunate—the recipient of good things. It conveys a sense of well-being that results from confidence in the LORD.

But there is one more observation that could be easily overlooked. Jeremiah addressed his audience with a word that emphasizes a certain characteristic. He used a word that describes someone who is brave or willing to take a risk. The statement can be translated this way:

"Blessed is the brave person whose hope is in the LORD and whose hope is the LORD."

I suppose that *any* hope is a risky venture—particularly hope in the LORD. Releasing the grip on self-determination may be easy in theory, but it is quite difficult in practice. As much as we would like to tell ourselves that we're enough, there's a voice within us that whispers from the shadows of our thoughts that we're doomed to failure. It's a risk to look beyond ourselves and center our hope on someone else. It *is* a risk, but it's *wise* risk.

PURSUING HOPE

- Where do you feel the greatest uncertainty in your life?

- In what ways do you want God to alter those areas of uncertainty?

- How is it possible for the LORD, Himself, to be the fulfillment of our hope?

PRACTICING HOPE

- Memorize Jeremiah 17:7. Try to explain this verse to one other person.

- Personalize Jer. 17:7, in prayer to the LORD.

- Experiment with the risk of Jeremiah's statement by weaving these 3-word prayers into every aspect of your day, addressing them to Yahweh, the God of your redemption.
  "I adore You"
  "LORD have mercy"
  "Into Your hands"

PERSONAL NOTES

looking beyond ourselves

4

BETWEEN TWO REALITIES

"I recall this to my mind, therefore I have hope"
Lamentations 3:21

T he average person processes between 25,000 and 75,000 thoughts per day. The vast majority of those thoughts are repetitious and we may not even be aware of them. The remainder is what we commonly refer to as self talk—the continuous conversation we have with ourselves in which we process our experience of life. In this mental chatter we evaluate others and ourselves and life itself. It is here that we rehearse what we believe and decide our actions. So how does this relate to hope?

Because hope is an attachment to the future, it needs cords of information that tie it to the present. In the grip of our thoughts, the anticipation of the future can pull us through anything this life offers. But if we let go of those cords, if we stop dwelling on what is true, hope vanishes like a dream. Telling ourselves the truth about where the story is going and how it's going to get there is what activates hope in the present.

One of the more dramatic expressions of this is found in a long, haunting poem written in response to a devastating event—the destruction of Jerusalem in 586 BC. Jeremiah, the prophet, was an eyewitness of the event. The images in the prophet's memory capture a wide range of the human experience: loss, pain, confusion, injustice, and uncertainty. The cruel reality before him was overwhelming and begged for relief, something to grasp when all else seemed trivial and useless. As he records for us the conversation within himself, he begins by acknowledging the harsh realities of his experience. He feels alone, bitter and distant from God. His thoughts are dominated by a sense of defeat and he concedes, "inevitably my soul rehearses these realities and is drug down with me."[3]

---

[3] Lamentations 3:20

So how does Jeremiah deal with this hope deficit?

The poet begins with *"This I recall."* When all the trinkets of hope (the fools gold and illusions of security) had been removed, he brought back to mind what was most real. He chose what he would think about, what he would tell himself was true. There was no denial of life's present experience, but something else was *also* true. One was unavoidable, the other was undeniable. "This I recall," he wrote, "therefore I have hope."

Our experience of hope is not automatic. It hinges on what we are telling ourselves is true—the inner dialogue we have with ourselves, that unheard conversation continuously going on within us … sometimes in the background, sometimes as a conscious activity. We *choose* what we will tell ourselves is true.

So what is it that Jeremiah chooses to dwell upon? What is the greater reality that will occupy his thoughts? He tells us.

"The LORD'S lovingkindnesses indeed never cease,for His compassions never fail. They are new every morning.

Great is Your faithfulness!"[4]

In other words, he says, "Because YOU are real, strong, able, loving, wise, in control, all-knowing, all-powerful and have a good purpose in mind … I need not fear. All is well. I can rest in you."

What is remarkable is that the prophet called those realities to his attention even when there was no tangible evidence of them. Life appeared to deny those claims. It would have been far easier to sing these lines in times of prosperity, when days were filled with laughter and promise. But he takes it a step further when he writes:

"The LORD is my portion, says my soul,
  therefore I have hope in Him."[5]

As he speaks to himself within his soul, he clarifies that his hope is not in the outcome, but in the Person who determines the outcome. Jeremiah settles his mind with a reality larger than his experience. Twice he repeats the assertion, *The LORD is my portion.* Jeremiah concludes that He is enough, *more*

---

[4] Lamentations 3:22-23
[5] Lamentations 3:24

than enough, to satisfy the longings of his heart and settle his troubled soul. Our daily experience of hope is dependent on us arriving at that same conclusion.

Jeremiah's account of hope lost and reclaimed is one of many. The Bible presents a composite record of our collective search for hope. The journey always leads to the same destination. It may be a wandering, meandering path but it always ends up at the same place. There is only one source of true hope and only one hope large enough to address all the fears and uncertainties of this life, to settle our soul and generate an honest optimism about what lies ahead. The stories of hope recorded in the Scriptures always lead to the God of Hope—to the person of Jesus. Arriving at this destination, the grand search comes to rest.

PURSUING HOPE

- What are some of the current realities in your life that occupy your thoughts?

- What are some of the other realities the Scriptures say are *also* true?

- Which list seems/feels more real to you today? Why?

PRACTICING HOPE

- Memorize Lamentations 3:21-24, emphasizing the personal pronouns.

- Personalize these verses as part of your prayer conversation with God.

- Try beginning your day by writing a journal entry that describes what Lamentations 3:21-24 will look like for you in that day.

PERSONAL NOTES

5

THE GRAND ESSENTIALS

"Now abide these three—faith, hope, love."
1 Corinthians 13:13

W hat would you say are the essentials of life? Depending on how you approach the question, you might think of objective needs like food, clothing and shelter. Or you might go with social values like freedom, peace and justice. Allan K Chalmers, a professor and activist in the 1960s, approached the question from the standpoint of enjoying life. He concluded that the grand essentials of happiness are "something to do, something to love, and *something to hope for*." He recognized that happiness in this life requires something that calls us forward; an anticipation of something desired; a longing that makes us look to what lies ahead—hope.

The Apostle Paul wrote that there are three "grand essentials" at the core of the Christian experience—faith, hope, love. His powerful manifesto on love concludes with this statement:

> "Now abide these three—**faith, hope, love**."

Another way of saying that might be, "Here are three enduring features of life" or "When all is said and done, these three remain." Paul is calling attention to what truly matters in this life. In the middle of that short list is *hope*. It's more than a mere hyphen between faith and love. It's one of the grand essentials.

Now, it may be that you're thinking (as I did) that this may be nothing more than a poetic way for Paul wrap up his thoughts and make a point. And you may be right … except that this triad appears elsewhere. For example, Paul also weaves them into his description of the hallmark features of Christian living. He praises believers in the Greek city of Thessalonica by writing:

> "We are constantly bearing in mind your work of **faith** and labor of **love** and steadfastness of

hope in our Lord Jesus Christ."[6]

Did you notice how Paul crafts this statement? He says there is work associated with faith and labor associated with love? But it sounds like hope may be what lightens the weight, focuses the efforts and replenishes the energy that is expended. In another place, Paul uses the imagery of Roman armor to describe our defenses against the enemy of our soul. He writes:

> "Let us be clear-minded, having put on the breastplate of **faith** and **love**, and as a helmet, the **hope** of salvation."[7]

Here again, hope is one of the three essentials, and yet distinguished from the other two. Faith and love are pictured as a breastplate, guarding the heart—the very core of our being. But hope is depicted as a helmet, protecting the head, where we process life and decide how to navigate through its challenges.

Bottom line: hope is a key feature of our redemption in Jesus. The New Testament

---

[6] 1 Thessalonians 1:3
[7] 1 Thessalonians 5:8

speaks of hope more than 120 times. It's referred to as an anchor for our soul and a cause of rejoicing. Peter (one of the apostles) calls us to be ready to give an account for the *hope* that is in us. Hope is a necessary component for understanding the narrative that now defines our lives in Jesus—that larger story of redemption that both precedes us and is yet to be completed.

However, when hope is paired with faith and love, it seems to fade into the background and lose its weight. We have considered hope itself as psychological/emotional currency and contemplated its significance in our lives. But let's take a moment to differentiate it from faith and love, and consider some of its unique identity.

First of all, I would suggest that faith emphasizes *what* we believe, while hope emphasizes *how* we believe. Let's think about this at bit more. What we truly desire, we hope for. We dream of it and anticipate possessing it. It is possible to believe many things and long for none of them. Simply because we believe (at least in theory) that something is true, it doesn't mean that we are emotionally connected to it. Hope is an emotional response to what we believe—it expresses a longing of the heart.

It is somewhat easier to distinguish hope from love. One contrast might be that love links faith to the present, while hope links it to the future. Both faith and love demand practical expression in daily life. Hope fuels those expressions by providing the narrative for the work of faith and the labor of love.

So here's how it works. Faith provides the content for hope, informing us about realities that change how we see this life. Hope then provides a context for love—one that is actively aware of, and emotionally connected to, a larger story that is playing out. Operating together, faith, hope and love comprise the "Grand Essentials" of the Christian life.

PURSUING HOPE

- What are you counting on to be true in the future in order to feel confident in the present?

- What goals are you living toward?

- Where do you believe the story is going?

PRACTICING HOPE

- Memorize 1 Corinthians 13:13, and repeat it to yourself throughout the day.

- Imagine yourself enacting 1 Thessalonians 5:8.

- Begin assembling a file of biblical verses that address hope.

PERSONAL NOTES

6

Now & Not Yet

"In hope we have been saved"
Romans 8:24

E very great story is a story of redemption, and every story of redemption begins with a crisis. Somehow life comes apart and our fallen nature is exposed once again. Without such a crisis, the story would have no context. But by itself, the story is incomplete and the characters are hopelessly suspended in a mystery that demands resolution. Something within us longs for the story to move on. We wonder how the crisis will be resolved.

The significance of a story is not in how it begins, but in how it ends. A story of redemption must begin with some failure or tragedy from which to be redeemed. Although our darker side may be captivated by the vulgar details of the starting point, something deep inside us searches for hope in the story that follows.

In a letter to the believers in first-century Rome, the Apostle Paul describes the state of this world and presents a brief synopsis of the story from the perspective of a much larger narrative—God's grand story of redemption. Paul does this in the form of an analogy. He pictures all of creation in the throws of childbirth and desperately longing for what is yet to come. The graphic imagery is filled with wrenching pain and deep emotion. There is sweat and groans and an urgency that cries out for release. But as intense as it is, the analogy is not one of despair, but of hope.

Paul saturates the imagery with a profound awareness of what is, and what is yet to come. There is something that is already true, but not yet fully revealed. It's in the pairing of these two, the now and not yet, that hope takes on a new dynamic. Paul concludes his analogy with this statement:

> "For in **hope** we have been saved, but **hope** that is seen is not really **hope**; for who **hopes** for what he already sees? But if we **hope** for what we do not see,

with perseverance we eagerly wait for it."[8]

"In **hope** *we have been saved."* It should not surprise us that hope is presented as a central feature of new life in Christ. Hope is the activating term for much of what defines this good news. The Scriptures speak of the *hope* of His calling[9], the *hope* of the Gospel[10], the *hope* of glory[11], the *hope* of salvation[12] and the *hope* of eternal life[13]. This hope is a watershed distinction of faith in Christ. We are told that prior to encountering new life in Christ, we are without *hope* and without God, and that after such an encounter we should be prepared to offer a reason for the *hope* that is now in us. So ... hope should be part of what defines us.

Profound Absence

"hope *that is seen is not really* **hope;** *for who* **hopes** *for what one already sees?"* We don't hope

---

8 Romans 8:24-5
9 Ephesians 1:18
10 Colossians 1:23
11 Colossians 1:27
12 1 Thessalonians 5:8
13 Titus 3:7

for what we already have. Something must be missing and its absence inescapable. There is something deep and penetrating about our sense of the absent. The Scriptures make it clear that life, as we know it, is not life as God intended it to be. And if we're honest, we feel this to be true. God did not intend for life to be hollow and unfulfilled. He did not intend for us to occupy our lives with desperate attempts to stuff the emptiness with earthly packing material.

Hope embraces the reality that what is missing will be fulfilled. Most of what God has done in and for us lies in the future. We have a taste of it now, but its reality is yet unseen. We anticipate a day when Jesus will be physically present, when he will set things right, when we will be revealed for who we are in Christ. This is the good news that has been announced. In hope, we long for its delivery like we long for the conclusion of an epic novel.

Passionate Waiting

It appears that hope can be measured by the emotion of our anticipation and the extent to which that emotion alters how we approach life and respond to its emptiness. Paul wrote, *"with perseverance we eagerly wait."* This statement suggests an active determination toward what is presently absent, an intentional shifting of our emotional weight toward the future.

We may all have some vague, haunting sense that something is missing from this life, some elusive element that would tie it all together. But once we discover what is missing, once it has been revealed to us, it becomes the longing of the heart. We dream about it, talk about, imagine what it will be like. We bank on it. So...

"with perseverance we eagerly wait"

PURSUING HOPE

- What do you believe you are missing out on in this life?

- How would you describe this feeling of absence?

- How does a sense of absence affect how you see the future?

PRACTICING HOPE

- Memorize Romans 8:24-25.

- Make a list of what will be different when Jesus reigns.

- Talk with God about how the list you just made might affect your responses to life today.

PERSONAL NOTES

7

A COUNTER-INTUITIVE DISCOVERY

"We exult in our tribulations"
Romans 5:2-5

M ost of us consider hope to be a necessary response to the pain and struggles of life. When life beats us down, hope is what keeps us from giving up and caving in. That glimmer of possibility gives us the courage to persevere, to endure, to survive. But what if the brokenness of this world is not just something to be endured? What if all the pain and struggle and disappointment are serving a larger purpose?

In response to those questions, consider this statement from a letter written by the Apostle Paul. It's addressed to believers who were facing the same realities that we face today.

> "We exult in the hope of God's glory. And not only this, but we

> also exult in our tribulations,
> knowing that tribulation brings
> about perseverance; and
> perseverance, proven character;
> and proven character, hope."[14]

Paul begins this statement by focusing our attention on our ultimate future—the hope of God's glory. However, the idea of some distant glory can seem irrelevant as we stare into the uncaring present. Such hope seems to be dangled as a prize a little too far away. Over time we can easily become bitter, angry and profoundly disappointed with life. It's understandable that life in this broken world will take its toll on us—more on some than others. So how can we orient ourselves in such a way that we acknowledge the realities of life without allowing them to drag us beneath their dark weight?

Paul's statement offers an alternative to bitterness and resentment. He calls us to not only cherish the prize of hope, but also the *process* for attaining it. He begins with darker words like tribulation and perseverance as a prelude to the lighter tones of discovery and

---

[14] Romans 5:2-5

hope. Paul says the journey begins in the messiness of life, the unavoidable pressures and pains and traumas of our common reality. They include all of those experiences that we try to avoid or escape. They're what we pray will pass quickly and never return.

I appreciate that this statement does not diminish our experiences of life. Quite the contrary; it validates them and adds value to them. This is important, because we have a different coping power if we're convinced that whatever we are going through is worth something, that it's not merely meaningless pain and random happenings. In these few lines we find insight into how we can make some sense of the painful features of life as we know them today—the throbbing state of things that cannot be ignored.

According to Paul's equation, our tribulations cultivate perseverance. Another way of saying that is that the continual trauma of life forces us to live with the present while longing for something better. Tribulations diminish the fantasies of self-reliance and ultimate victory over the brokenness that plagues this world.[15] It's the pain of the present that makes us look to the future.

Paul points out that such determined waiting leads to proven character. In other words, it forces us to work out the content of our faith, putting to the test everything we claim to believe. It is in this crucible of life that our faith moves from theory to reality, forming the substance of our hope and a different experience of life. Paul says it this way:

> "and hope does not disappoint,
> because the love of God has been
> poured out within our hearts
> through the Holy Spirit who was
> given to us."

What does Paul mean when he says that hope does not disappoint? Good question. It may help to know that the Greek word translated here as "disappoint" is more often used to express the idea of shame or humiliation. In this case it carries the weight of a profound disgrace that comes from having one's hope shown to be in vain—ones

---

[15] See 2 Corinthians 1:8-10

currency worthless. Paul may be alluding to this shame when he says, "If we have hoped in Christ in this life only, we are of all men most to be pitied."[16] In other words, eventually, whatever you have counted on to be true in the future will be revealed for what it is.

So what about now? Where do we find the emotional courage for the present? Paul's conclusion brings us back to our future hope, but with a very personal connection. He writes, "because the love of God *has been* poured out within our hearts." We already have the centerpiece of our hope—God's love.

God has not left us alone to beat our way through the harsh realities of this life. He does not stoically say to us, "Hey, I know this life is tough. But stick with it, slug it out, and I'll wait for you on the other side of the finish line." On the contrary, He is intensely present with us *now*, pouring out His love within our hearts. God does not take our pain and suffering lightly. Every experience in this life has eternal value in God's economy.

---

[16] 1 Corinthians 15:19

So it seems that the trauma of this world is actually beneficial to all who have found redemption in Christ. The very hope that carries us through this fallen world is formed and shaped by its brokenness.

PURSUING HOPE

- What does "tribulation" look like for you?

- What does "perseverance" look like in that tribulation?

- How might God be pouring out His love within your heart at this very moment?

PRACTICING HOPE

- Describe your tribulation in poetic language by writing your own psalm.

- Draw an abstract image to represent your psalm.

- Rewrite Romans 5:2-5 in your own words, personalizing it as you write.

PERSONAL NOTES

a counter-intuitive discovery

8

WHEN DARKNESS SEEMS TO RULE

"You were without hope"
Ephesians 2:12

O ur spring almanac is sprinkled with largely overlooked days having obscure names like Ash Wednesday, Maundy Thursday and Palm Sunday. Although they may show up on our calendars, they receive smaller billing and tend to serve only as reminders that the headliner event, Easter, is drawing near. One of these days seems conspicuously misnamed—Good Friday.

For those who experienced that day up close, there was nothing "good" about it. It was a day saturated with brutality, fear and confusion. Their world had literally grown dark and the ground had trembled beneath their feet. I wonder if some felt foolish for having placed all of their hopes in the one who now hung in public shame on the outskirts of town. I wonder if some who had been delivered from demons now feared their return. Perhaps some recalled a better time when they watched a young girl return from the dead and gasp her first breath of air. Maybe others remembered a blind man blinking with astonishment at his first sight of life, or a crippled woman dancing with delight, or a terminally diseased man showing off his perfectly healed hands. There were many other Fridays that were good, but not this one.

Firsthand accounts describe a scene of chaos among the followers of the dead rabbi—running, hiding, fearing for their lives. Their association with the great teacher from Galilee had marked them as traitors and heretics. The one who had spoken words of life was now silent and they panicked at the possibilities of what might now happen to them. There was no apparent "good" on that day; it was a day of despair—a day when all hope was lost.

On that day, the central feature was a cruel instrument of death, an effective tool for the execution of criminals. The cross was a common sight throughout the Roman

Empire. But that day was different and that cross unique, for on it hung the hope of the world. On that day, the drama that played out was not only an indictment of humanity, but also a fulfillment of promises made before the foundation of the world.

On that day, sin was fully exposed in all its grotesque violence and insidious corruption. A fallen world retched evil from its deepest bowels. God unleashed His legitimate anger; His creation had been violated, poisoned with evil. On that day the earth shook with God's deep grief, profound disappointment and unendurable hurt as a father watched his child die. The wail of God's pain was voiced on that day.

But Good Friday was not an accident. It's not simply a story of betrayal and political oppression. It's not merely the tragic account of a good man dying as a martyr. It was, instead, a vital piece of a larger story. Father and Son had anticipated that day from the beginning of time. Jesus never lost sight of it. He spoke of it clearly and often, saying such things as, "For this reason I came."[17]

---

[17] John 12:27 and 18:37

I believe we need to linger at the base of a cross with our Redeemer still upon it and absorb the reality of what happened on that day. The cross is proof that we are guilty. We must resist moving past that day too quickly for our understanding of Easter is dependent on our understanding of Good Friday.

But I also believe that the Cross is indisputable evidence of God's love.; not a soft, cuddly love but a love that is deep, fierce and scandalous. The Cross is tangible proof of forgiveness. Sin has been disposed—it's over!

On that day, and on any day when darkness seems to rule, what appeared to destroy all hope was actually the fulfillment of real hope. It was indeed Good Friday.

PURSUING HOPE

- Imagine yourself present on that dark Friday when Jesus died. Imagine the despair of those days immediately before His resurrection. What would you have longed for most?

- Remember one of the darkest days in your life. What did that feel like? What did you long for most?

- How can knowing the larger story change how you experience dark days?

PRACTICING HOPE

- Imagine yourself at the foot of the Cross.

- Read "Dark Night of The Soul" by John of the Cross

- Encourage someone who is going through a dark time. Write that person a note or speak to them face-to-face. Then take your own encouragement to heart.

PERSONAL NOTES

when darkness seems to rule

9

A LIVING HOPE

"reborn into a living hope"
1 Peter 1:3

So I'm here at my desk on the week after Easter. It was a wonderful weekend with family, friends and neighbors—lots of laughter and celebration, good food and meaningful conversation. But now the events have passed and as I wake up to the everyday, one statement continues to hold my attention ... *"a living hope."*

If Friday was marked by horrific death and crippling despair, then Sunday was the polar opposite. It was a day charged with adrenaline—running and shouting, terrified soldiers and shocked mourners. Sunday's first light was announced by the deep rumble of a violent earthquake. The dramatic appearance of the risen King unhinged the city and altered the history of mankind. Both days were filled with startling announcements—one an unexpected death and the other an unbelievable life. One announcement sent the disciples into hiding; the other sent them into the streets. Peter, one of the eyewitnesses of that day later wrote these words.

> "Blessed be the God and Father of our Lord Jesus Christ, who according to His great mercy has caused us to be reborn into a living hope through the resurrection of Jesus Christ from the dead."[18]

As I have turned this statement over in my mind and allowed it to steep in my imagination, the words "living hope" have stood out as if in bold print. According to this ancient text, the evidence of God's great mercy and the wonderful consequence of Jesus' resurrection is the restart of life in the form of a living hope. But what actually is this *living* hope; and how is it different from any other hope?

---

[18] 1 Peter 1:3

The first and most obvious answer is that the very source of our hope, Jesus, is alive. The one we are counting on as the hero of the story (of *our* story) is a living person in real time. Our hope is not simply in the memory of a person who has passed away and has nothing more to offer us than some tips for positive living. It's a *living* hope because Jesus is alive. This is the essence of the Gospel—the good news that Jesus lived, died and physically rose again from the grave exactly as the Scriptures said he would.[19] Everything hangs on this one event.[20] It's also a *living* hope because Jesus raising from the dead offers us absolute assurance (proof) that what we are banking on is a sure bet. Life in this broken, fallen world is not terminal. There is hope beyond the grave. And if that's true, then there is also hope on this side of the grave.

For those who experienced that day when Jesus reappeared, everything changed. That which had been too good to be true became too real to be ignored. The physical presence of Jesus provided tangible evidence that the source of their hope was real.

---

[19] 1 Corinthians 15:1-8
[20] 1 Corinthians 15: 12-19

Their confidence had not been in His words alone, but in His ability to fulfill those words. While He was present with them, that hope was secure. But when He died, it was as if their "hope account" had been hacked and drained to zero, then discovering that they were suddenly bankrupt and their creditors were calling in their debts. But now all debts had been paid in full and their "hope checks" secured forever.

The term "living" not only points to an objective reality—Jesus is alive—but also to a more subjective one. Consider this: we all ask a common set of questions as we travel through this life.[21] We ask them in our own vernacular and recast them as we encounter each new chapter of our story, but the questions are consistent and universal. Some of those questions address the purpose of life—What is it? Why am I doing what I'm doing? Where does it all lead? How we answer those questions is foundational to how we order our lives. "Hope" is the label on the mental folder that holds our answers to those questions. Hope is a word that captures what

---

[21] Other questions were considered in chapter one.

we see of value ahead of us, what adds purpose to our future and calls us toward it.

Because of what happened on Easter Sunday, the folder can now hold a different kind of hope. Peter deliberately chose to describe this hope as "living." It's a word that references a divergent kind of life, an uncommon experience of life. Living conveys the idea of being active, real and relevant as opposed to stagnant, academic and lifeless. Such a description associates this hope with the living Word[22] and living water[23]. The words "born into" indicate that this living hope launches a new beginning, a certain kind of existence that was not possible before. *Living hope* is the great prize won on Easter Sunday.

On this week after Easter, I'm dwelling on two insights. *First:* This living hope does not source from me and how well I order my life, but from God's great mercy and a cataclysmic event that changes everything. *Second:* The hope we have been born into is both life-giving and life-sustaining. It pulses within us, marking the cadence of its eternal source. It

---

[22] Hebrews 4:12
[23] John 4:10-14

provides an alternative answer for the purpose of this life and a dramatic shift to what animates it.

PURSUING HOPE

- Imagine yourself in Jerusalem on the day Jesus rose from the grave. Imagine hearing the news of this event for the first time. As one who had followed Jesus and witnessed his execution, how do you think the news would affect you? What thoughts might run through your mind?

- How would you answer the "common questions" mentioned above? What do your answers say about your hope?

- How would you describe "living hope" to someone else?

PRACTICING HOPE

- Memorize 1 Peter 1:3, emphasizing the words "living hope."
- Complete the following statement. "Because I have a living hope, I _____." Find five ways to complete the statement.

- Decide what living hope will look like in your life today.

PERSONAL NOTES

a living hope

10

MISSING PIECES

"Christ in you, the hope of glory"
Colossians 1:27

One of the frustrations in this life (in addition to waiting) is that the individual pieces of it don't seem to add up. There is no sure-fire way to successfully run the gauntlet of life and avoid the pain and tragedy of a fallen world. No matter how carefully we chart our course, "life happens" and we have to adjust and continue with life as it presents itself. We try to make sense of it, but without a larger narrative beyond our own small story, we inevitably find ourselves hope impaired.

Something is missing. It's like a jigsaw puzzle in which key pieces have been stuffed into someone's pocket. What's worse, it's like the image on its box cover that has been distorted to portray what we might desire the finished puzzle looks like; an image more to our liking rather than to the true picture.

The biblical terminology for those missing pieces (and the true image on the box cover) is *mystery*. In biblical parlance, mystery referred to what was hidden from view—concealed from common knowledge and collective wisdom. A mystery often referred to a secret that explained a riddle or unlocked a unsolvable question. But here's the catch ... a mystery could not be discovered. It had to be disclosed.

Mysteries beg questions. Some of those questions focus on the immediate—Why is this happening to me? What's going on? Other questions address much larger mysteries—What's this life about? Where is all of this heading?[24] Philosophers have chased these questions for millennia and still we are left with mysteries.

The Apostle Paul picks up this language of mystery and lays the missing pieces on the table. He writes to those who were trying to make sense of life and discloses the secret. He addresses "the mystery which has been hidden

---

[24] These questions have been mentioned in chapters __ and __.

from the past ages and generations, but has now been made known."[25] The mystery is captured in a single phrase:

"Christ in you, the hope of glory."

This simple statement unlocks virtually every mystery of life. It speaks to the jumbled confusion of the present, as well as those larger ultimate issues of purpose and destiny. Although it may not seem to be the missing piece we are searching for and although it raises a host of additional questions, Paul discloses that all the mysteries of life find their resolution in these few words.

"Christ in you"

The mystery is not merely stated in one word—Jesus. It is instead a far more intimate language that is used—Christ in you. The death and resurrection of Jesus is what brings power to this statement, and a contrastive way of living is the consequence. These few words reveal a new dynamic operating within those who have found redemption in Jesus. The intimate presence of Jesus *within* us changes everything.

---

[25] Colossians 1:26

How? What actually changes? This hidden insight is not a promise that circumstances will change for the better. It's not a secret pass to an easier life. However, the awareness of Jesus' presence within us, in the core of our being, activates the mystery in practical terms. His presence dispels fear and calms our soul. His presence confirms the reality that we are truly His. His presence fills our emptiness with His fullness. But one of the most powerful consequences of His presence is hope.

"the hope of glory"

The *hope of glory* may sound distant and unrelated to the routines of life. However, this simple phrase is what creates a larger narrative in which to define our story and gives meaning to all the seemingly random pieces of our lives. This phrase points to something outside the smallness of our perception, a longing within us that seemed unattainable. It puts a picture on the puzzle box and makes sense of the strangely shaped pieces.

The actual "mystery" is found in the person of Jesus—who He is and what He has done. Jesus has not only died the death we should have died, but has also lived the life we should be living. Because of His life within us, we can experience the hope of something far greater—the hope of glory. The phrase speaks of things being put right, of us being put right. When the pieces are all put in place, the picture is one of grace and mercy. It's a complex picture, made up of a thousand experiences and millions of moments. It's a picture of Christ in us and the hope of glory … experienced.

PURSUING HOPE

- In what ways has the phrase "life happens" been showing up in your life?

- What questions do you find yourself asking as life happens and you find yourself in the midst of its complexities?

- In what ways can the mystery of "Christ in you" change how we perceive what is happening?

PRACTICING HOPE

- Complete these statements:
(1) Because Christ is in me, I am ___.
(2) Because Christ is in me, I can ___ .
(3) Because Christ is in me, I will ___ .

- Write a concluding paragraph to your own autobiography, describing how the mystery of "Christ in you" became a reality in you.

- Imagine how your life might be when all is put right.

PERSONAL NOTES

11

AN ANCHOR FOR THE SOUL

"This hope we have as an anchor for the soul"
Hebrews 6:19

L iving in Santa Cruz, California, one of our favorite places to walk is along a path that traces the northern cliff-edged point of the Monterey Bay. Some days the view is idyllic—peaceful, blue water with gentle swells slowly approaching the land's edge. We love to bask in the warmth of sunny, pleasant days. But there are other days when the water reflects the dark grays of the sky and pummels the cliffs with thunderous waves. That northern point of the bay is marked by a rocky protrusion and a picturesque lighthouse. On stormy days, powerful waves slam that prominent point and the force of their assault explodes skyward in a spectacular plume of white water.

The ocean provides a graphic metaphor of life as we experience it, with all of its moods and movement, its unexpected changes and endless variations. The writer of Hebrews uses this imagery, picturing our souls upon a vast sea of uncertainty.

"the soul"

The soul is a very human term. It refers to that inner, unseen part of us that interacts with life and animates our actions. It's where we try to make sense of life. There are times when our soul is at rest and the seas of our emotions are calm. But there are other times when there is such turmoil within us that we feel in danger of sinking into the depths of despair. In the Psalms, David often refers to the soul as agitated, oppressed, besieged, gasping, struggling, disturbed, troubled. Into such a reality, the Scriptures present hope as an anchor that secures our drifting souls to solid ground. In a world of uncertainty and instability, we are rescued by these words:

> "This hope we have as an anchor for the soul"[26]

---

[26] Hebrews 6:19

This imagery reveals something about us and about our hope. It seems to indicate that our soul, left alone, is restless and at risk. The very need for an anchor speaks to our soul floating as a ship on the sea, at the mercy of the elements—currents, winds and waves.

There are times when we may feel like a person clinging to a piece of flotsam in a roiling, empty ocean with no help on the horizon. Nothing is stable or secure. We feel defenseless against the powerful currents— forces beyond our control that drag us away. Winds that churn the sea toss us about. Even in the best of times, we may feel disoriented, confused, unsettled and aimless.

We're not necessarily shipwrecked or abandoned, just lost with our mooring lines hanging limp in the water. There's a sense of being disconnected from anything truly secure. We may tell ourselves to be brave; that life is tough and we must be strong. True. But still we find ourselves searching the horizon for something … anything.

"This hope we have as an anchor for the soul, a hope both sure and steadfast"

The anchor is described with words

97

intended to calm our emotions and quiet our desperate thoughts. It is sure and steadfast. These words convey the ideas of safety, security and strength; of being connected to what is solid and permanent. In a world where nothing is certain, the soul longs for such stability.

The writer has a specific hope in mind: "this" hope. He connects *this* hope to the unchangeableness of God's purpose and the guarantee of God's oath. Both of these, he writes, find bedrock in the character of God and the record of His faithfulness.

The analogy of an anchor brings a couple of thoughts to mind. First, an anchor does not calm the sea or clear the skies, but it does provide security in the midst of it all. The gales continue to blow and the waves threaten to tear us away. Currents are always tugging. Our line to the anchor is never slack or untested.

A second thought that emerges from the anchor analogy speaks to a mystery. For an anchor to have its affect, it must be dropped below the surface, deep into what cannot be seen. The anchor finds its mooring in a hidden reality. In a similar way, our soul finds its security in an unseen reality.

Take a moment to picture someone lost at sea. How would that person's expressions, actions, demeanor and chances for survival be affected by whether they have hope of rescue … or not? How would it change:

- If they believe someone may come for them.

- If they believe someone *will* come for them.

- If they believe someone is coming and all will turn out well.

- Or… if they believe no one is coming and they are utterly alone and lost.

The point is this: If Jesus is our hope, then he's not merely our wishful thought, our last resort or our best chance at winning. Actually, Jesus is both the anchor AND the bedrock. He is the intensely present help when we feel alone, the one who guarantees the future when all seems at risk, the one who calms the soul that is bound to Him.

PURSUING HOPE

- Apart from Christ, what alternatives does one have for calming the soul?

- At this point in your life, are you more susceptible to drift or distress? Why?

- How might the hope presented in Hebrews 6:17-20 provide "strong encouragement" for you?

PRACTICING HOPE

- Rewrite Hebrews 6:17-20 in your own words.

- Imagine your life anchored to the hope described in Hebrews 6:17-20. How would this alter your experience of this day?

- Devise three ways you can anchor your soul to hope today.

PERSONAL NOTES

12

HOPE AGAINST HOPE

"In hope against hope he believed"
Romans 4:18

Sometimes, perhaps often, it's easier to hope for something that's within the realm of possibility, something we know is possible. It may seem more assuring to hope for some scenario that makes sense in the world as we know it.

Much of our common everyday hope falls into this category. For example, we may hope for a job. After all, we are well qualified and have good references. We may hope to get over a bad experience, reasoning that better days are coming and that time heals most things. Or we may hope to make it through a bout with some health issue with the help of good doctors and medication. It's much more convenient to hope for a certain outcome when we can imagine a reasonable pathway to that end. But what if what we hope for seems impossible?

Those who place their faith in Jesus are to be known by their hope. However, what is hoped for defies the laws of nature and the wisdom of this world. The great hope that defines salvation is not found in the new job or the recovery from a painful experience. It's a hope that anticipates an entirely divergent scenario—something impossible. As life plays itself out we may feel like we are *hoping against hope*. The expression finds its origin in an ancient letter written by Paul to the believers in Rome. He tells the story of the aging Abraham, patriarch of the Old Testament, and writes,

"In hope against hope he believed"

Abraham was a man who left everything on the basis of an angel's second-hand message from God. He faithfully followed and worshipped this God through the prime of his life and arrived in the graying years as wealthy man. He had known more drama and adventure than most ever dream of. Yet one promise remained unfulfilled—he had no son.

The one promise that mattered most to him in his closing years seemed empty.

Abraham's story would have been completely different if his wife Sarah had become pregnant a few weeks after the promise was delivered ... still amazing, but different. It's that difference that makes the account even more powerful as it comes to us.

Not only does the biblical narrative present us with too-good-to-be-true realities, it casts them with built-in drama—the element of waiting. And it's not just a matter of waiting, but of delay that offers no evidence that the promises are true. Life continues as it did before. Sarah remained barren ... for years. The longer the promise remained unfulfilled, the less chance there was that the Promiser would make good on His word. Time was running out.

"In hope against hope he believed"

The expression may sound familiar to us. It means to believe that something will happen, even when everything seems to indicate it won't. It could be put many other ways: Continuing to hope when all logic defies it; Holding on to a possibility when there is no chance of it happening; Refusing to give in to the way things appear; Continuing to hope when one seems to be abandoned by hope; Hope that has little or no supporting evidence. Whichever way we choose to say it, the expression carries the same weight.

In Paul's letter, the expression is nested between two statements that bring it alive. The statement that follows the phrase reveals that Abraham counted on a specific promise. He had been lead to believe that he would become the father of many nations. It was the singular mark of a life-changing covenant God had made with him. The promise was intimately wrapped up in his very identity. His name had been changed from "Abram" to fully identify him with the promise[27] and He was now "Abraham"—father of a multitude. The validity of the covenant hung in the fulfillment of the promise. Twenty years passed while God remained silent. And yet…

So what kept this hope alive? The answer is provided in the words that lead into the phrase. Abraham believed in a God who "gives life to the dead and calls into being that

---

[27] Genesis 17:1-5

which does not exist."

Abraham not only counted on a specific promise, he counted on a specific God. Apart from its source, the promise was ridiculous, unbelievable—the delusional thinking of an old man.

One of the distinguishing marks of the hope found in Jesus is that it is completely dependent upon the God who speaks it into existence. We anticipate its fulfillment in the face of all worldly wisdom to the contrary.

"Hope against hope" is not a statement of despair. It is a conscious decision to place hope in the God who speaks rather than the wisdom of the world. It is an accurate description of hope that finds its source outside the opaque limitations of this world.

God fulfilled His promise to Abraham. He always does. He always will.

PURSUING HOPE

- When are you most likely to feel like your hope is futile? In such times, what thoughts run through your mind?

- Why do you think God waited so long to fulfill His promise to Abraham?

- What kind of mental conversations do you believe Abraham had within himself during those years of waiting?

PRACTICING HOPE

- Invent your own private symbol for the phrase "hope against hope." Place the symbol where you will see it when you are most vulnerable to discouragement.

- Remind (reread) yourself of Romans 4:17 before you pray.

- List three things you are convinced to be true of God. Write them on a small piece of paper and slide it into your pocket. Every time your hand touches that paper consciously repeat those three lines to yourself.

PERSONAL NOTES

hope against hope

13

HERE & NOW

"I would have despaired unless I had believed"
Psalm 27:13

The storyline of David's early years may sound familiar to many. He was raised in a dysfunctional family, marginalized and minimized. Along the way, he discovered certain talents and skills that seemed to open doors for him and create opportunities. He was given promises of a bright future. There was hope.

But then life did what it often seems to do. Doors slammed and promises were lost in the confusing circumstances and unexpected twists in the story. Some of the people David counted on disappeared and others became his adversaries. His vision for the future lost its glamour and David found himself in a place of crisis. The one who would become Israel's most famous king was on the brink of despair.

It's not hard for us to find common ground with David. This snapshot of his experience may sound somewhat familiar to our own. Make a few adjustments and we could write ourselves into the script. One day we may have every reason to feel confident about the future and the next day find ourselves fearful of what lies ahead.

As David encountered the harsh realities of life, he found himself struggling to sustain his self-confidence. So what did David *do* in those spaces of uncertainty when his clear picture of the future had become blurred? How did he restore hope in the here-and-now when everything seemed to deny it?

The answer (at least some insight) may be found in a poem David wrote in one of those times. After laying out the longing of his heart in the initial lines of the poem, after expressing his disappointment and confusion, David writes these words:

"I would have despaired unless I had believed that I would see the goodness of the LORD in the land of the living."

It's interesting that David was not counting on God to fulfill his dreams or to make the story turn out as he had envisioned it. His hope was not in a specific outcome of his own making. Instead, David found a different counterbalance for his looming despair—the goodness of God. In other words, David was counting on God to be who He is and to do what He does. David was not demanding his own way, but choosing to look for evidence of God's goodness in how the story unfolded.

David had loaded his "hope account" with what he knew about God. He had filled it with the truth of the Scriptures and the experiences of God's faithfulness. Now it was time to draw upon that account—to bank on what he knew. The tipping point in David's thinking is found in what he writes next:

"Wait for the LORD. Be strong and let your heart take courage. Yes, wait for the LORD."[28]

This appears to be some of that self-talk we discussed earlier. In these few lines, there are a couple of insights that may help us in the here-and-now. The first is found in the repeated line: *wait for the Lord*. The word "wait" is a Hebrew term that might also be

---

[28] Psalm 27:14

rendered "hope." It conveys the imagery of someone lifting his or her head and straining to see what lies beyond the horizon. David reminds himself that this is a choice. Where he chooses to fix his gaze will determine how the story progresses. David tells himself to *wait* for the LORD.

Ah, but waiting isn't easy. There is an old Jewish prayer that David may have whispered himself: "O Lord, I know that Thou wilt help us; but wilt Thou help us *before* Thou wilt help us?"

A key is found in the line between the two "wait" statements. It begins with an action we take, "be strong," and is completed with something God provides—courage. It's as though David looks at himself in the mirror and shouts, "Hey! What are you thinking? Put your thoughts on what you know to be true!" There are times when waiting (hoping) requires us to take charge of our thoughts and cling to what we know is true. Otherwise fear will take over and write our story.

It's the latter part of the line that brings hope into the present tense. My translation reads "*and let your heart take courage.*" However, a literal translation of the Hebrew reads more like this: *and He shall instill courage to your heart.* David is counting on God to be present in his experience and to instill courage to his heart. Now courage does not alter the circumstances, but it does alter our response to those circumstances. Courage is the ability to face what frightens us. It is the inner strength to carry on in spite of danger or disapproval. It is strength in the face of pain or grief. Courage rescues our heart from the grip of circumstances and moves it into the hands of God.

PURSUING HOPE

- How would you describe the difference between discouragement and despair?

- What does the goodness of God look like in real time? How would you recognize it?

- How might seeing the goodness of God activate hope? ... or keep you from despair?

PRACTICING HOPE

- Try restating Psalm 27:13 as a positive proposition. In other words, "If ___, then ___."

- Pray for eyes to notice God's goodness as He presents it (rather than how I imagine it should be).

- Plan to make journal entries concerning evidence of God's goodness you noticed that day.

PERSONAL NOTES

hope

14

EMOTIONAL HOPE

*"Now may the God of hope fill you with all joy and
peace in believing, that you may abound in hope by
the power of the Holy Spirit."*
Romans 15:13

R uthie and I became fans of Warriors'
basketball during the 2015 playoff
season. Although we have other things to do,
we find ourselves unable to take our eyes off
the tense, fast-moving games. Each game has
its own dramas that play out as the time ticks
down to the final buzzer. A roiling uncertainty
generates the emotion for those few hours.
There is something at stake that we care
about enough to cheer toward our desired
end.

In a letter to the early church at Rome,
Paul made a point to cast hope in highly
emotional terms. He writes that when we find
new life in Jesus, we cheer toward a desired

end as we *"exult in hope of the glory of God"* (Rom. 5:2). In fact, one of our identifying marks should be that we are continuously *"rejoicing in hope"* (Rom. 12:12). Near the end of that letter Paul offers this blessing:

> "Now may the God of hope fill
> you with all joy and peace in
> believing, so that you will abound
> in hope by the power of the Holy
> Spirit."[29]

This blessing is about hope: the God of hope and the hope of the redeemed. The evidence of that hope is emotional—joy and peace.

The blessing begins and ends with God. He is both the Source and Sustainer of our hope. He is the One who fills us with joy and peace, and He is the One who causes our hope to flourish. Our only part in the equation is "believing." Our part is choosing to believe that He is who He says He is and that His Word is true, that He can be trusted with our lives and our future. It is here that we set ourselves up for either joy and peace, or worry

---

[29] Romans 15:13

and bitterness. Timothy Keller, a pastor in New York, observed "Worry is not believing that God will get it right, and bitterness is believing that God got it wrong."

Hope is activated by faith (believing). However, we can believe many things are true without having those beliefs move our heart. It is possible to have a faith that is merely intellectual, but not so with hope. Here's the difference. While faith regards something as true, hope expects something to happen because of what is true. Hope is a willful act of moving our focus to a future event... and cheering. I once heard it put this way: Faith is hearing the music from a distant land. Hope is dancing to it.

So once again I find myself asking some questions—What do I actually expect God to do in my life? What do I look forward to in the future because of what I believe is true? How does the hope of what lies ahead change how I live in the present? I believe Paul's blessing not only provokes these questions but also frames how we respond to them. Here's how:

1. Hope animates the present as it revels in a reality that is yet to come. In doing so, hope

transforms the routines of daily life into an emotional prelude. It transforms the fear of the unknown into a setting for a surprise ending. As we place our confidence in the God of hope and actively anticipate what He has in store, He fills us with joy.

2. Hope also brings a willingness to live with the present—peace in the midst of present realities. It's an internal confidence in the face of external chaos and confusion. Our hope is fueled by insider information that anticipates an outcome that seems too good to be true.

Hope battles against its arch enemy—fear. Fear can take over the storyline and write our future. It's a form of unintentional storytelling in our mind, vividly imagining plots and suspense, generating possible answers for the question of what will happen next. In one of her blogs, Michele Cushatt noted, "Fear thrives on three lies: (1) I am alone, (2) I am powerless, (3) I am without hope."[30] But the God of hope does not leave us alone and powerless. As we place our confidence in Him, he quiets our soul.

---

[30] Michele Cushatt, February 24, 2014
http://michelecushatt.com/to-live-in-the-not-knowing/

Paul prays that the source of our hope would saturate our souls with joy and peace; that God would infuse us with an emotional response to this life that confounds the world around us and provides evidence of a greater reality. It is He who fills us with joy and peace, and causes hope to flourish—to abound and overflow, to be more than enough, far beyond what is needed.

Although we know how the story (game) ends, it often feels uncertain. Mini-dramas play out and opposing forces battle as though victory was up for grabs. There is indeed something at stake; an outcome vastly greater than any basketball title, one that the God of hope has already won. It is an outcome that we care about enough to cheer.

PURSUING HOPE

- What emotions dominate your life today? Why?

- In Romans 15:13, what is our part and what is God's part?

- If your life was to end today, how would you wish you had lived?

PRACTICING HOPE

- Memorize Romans 15:13, but do so as a blessing upon yourself.

- Allow the imagery of the music quote to linger in your thoughts.

- Search for songs that go along with this chapter.

PERSONAL NOTES

hope

15

PROVOCATIVE HOPE

"a reason for the hope that is in you"
1 Peter 3:15

I t seems that everyone I know has some dominate characteristic that distinguishes them in my mind. For example, there are some I think of as creative or funny or easy to be around. There are others who come across as serious or confident or empathetic. Some are comfortable with life and others chronically frustrated. Some are like Charlie Brown, and others like Eeyore. We all have certain general traits that have come to define us and the life we live. When others think of us (which is probably less often than we imagine) certain images come to their mind that identify us from their perspective. The options may vary but they probably all fall into some common categories. There is some kind of personal profiling that we have earned; a reputation that speaks to what is true about us.

One of the distinguishing marks of those who have found new life in Jesus is (or should be) hope. It is to be observable rather than stifled and covert. It is attractive and appealing. It is graciously provocative, calling for an explanation from those who encounter its presence. The hope we find in Jesus is not simply an added dimension of our personality, but something that is *also* true about us. Such hope actually redefines our story, altering everything about us. It becomes the very atmosphere in which we move, shaping how we understand this life. It becomes the larger hope that recasts all of our smaller hopes.

The Apostle Peter speaks to this in a letter to believers who had been scattered throughout the Roman Empire, living as aliens in places with exotic names like Bithynia, Cappadocia and Galatia. As they attempt to work out their faith in a hostile environment, Peter offers this encouragement:

"Sanctify Christ as Lord in your hearts, always being ready to make a defense to everyone who asks you to give an

account for the hope that is in you, yet
with gentleness and reverence."[31]

Notice that the focal point is hope. They
are to be known for their hope and to be
prepared to account for it. But rather than
begin with how they should craft a response,
he points first to the source of their hope.
Peter tells them to set Jesus apart from all the
competing influences in their lives and
recognize Him as Lord (the one who rules and
the source of their hope) in the center of their
being.

The statement assumes that those around
us are observing our lives and appraising what
they see. They are either dismissing us as
irrelevant or fascinated by something unusual
and attractive. If our lives provoke no
response, then that probably means we fall
into the first category. In order to fall into the
second category, there must be an observable
hope marked by such qualities as confidence,
anticipation and joy.

Peter encourages them not only to be aware
of a watching world, but also to be actively

---

[31] 1 Peter 3:15

aware of their hope. They are to be "ready," not with canned answers or debate questions, but with a "defense" and an "account." In other words, they were to confidently walk into each day with a reasoned explanation for the hope that is in them as well as a personal story that brought it to life. They didn't need to have all the answers, but their answers had to be their own.

One of the most brilliant thinkers of the 17th century was the French philosopher Blaise Pascal. He was an inventor, mathematician and physicist. When he encountered Jesus in 1654, Pascal threw his intellectual energies into writing what he believed would be an airtight defense of the Gospel. The working title of his massive undertaking was *Pensées* (thoughts). Along the way, he made a personal discovery that profoundly affected the project. Pascal recorded his revelation in a much smaller book entitled *The Art of Persuasion*. In it, he points out that we can win an argument or debate without necessarily persuading someone. He wrote, "For every man is almost always led to believe not through proof, but through that which is attractive."

Now, a word of caution may be in order. I believe it would be easy to read this clip from Peter's letter as merely another tactic for evangelism. But what if the emphasis is really more about what happens in *us* as we rehearse the reason for the hope we possess? Could it be that the "defense" and the "account" are also for our own sake?

Peter wraps up his encouragement by urging his readers to respond to the watching world with gentleness and respect (the art of persuasion). They (we) are to engage a broken world with conversation that is both winsome and honest—with words of hope.

PURSUING HOPE

- Which words might others use to describe you? (be honest) What do those words say about your hope in Christ?

- How could the hope developed in this book redefine how you are living your life?

- Which of the three redefining features discussed in this chapter do you believe would be most powerful in your life today? Why?

PRACTICING HOPE

- Memorize 1 Peter 3:15, emphasizing the word "hope."

- Plan how you will approach this day in order to be known by the hope that is in you.

- Begin to prepare a response for those who ask you to give "a reason for the hope that is in you."

PERSONAL NOTES

hope

conclusion

Practicing Hope

*"to realize the full assurance of hope
until the end"*
Hebrews 6:11

P racticing hope may sound like a strange pairing of words. Hope tends to have more of a passive feel to it—something that operates in the background while we are going about the activities of life. But hope, if left unattended, tends to drift and dissipate, losing its power as an activating principle in our lives. Because of this, it would be prudent for us to consider certain practices that are essential to the vitality of our hope.

But before we go there, let's take a moment to summarize the conversations that have brought us to this point. I believe they could all be gathered within two big ideas that address (1) what we hope *in* and (2) what we hope *for*.

What we hope in. Everyone has hope in

something. What determines its value is not how much we hope, but in the source of our hope—what we are counting on to be true. We considered the metaphor of hope as psychological/emotional currency we carry in our pockets. The currency is only as good as what secures it. As followers of Jesus, our hope-currency is not at risk because it is sourced in the God of the Bible who is absolutely faithful.

What we hope for. Hope is the way we imagine the future based upon what we are counting on to be true. As followers of Jesus, not only are we counting on the God of hope to be who He is (faithful), but also to do what He has promised—both in the present and in the future. Our hope anticipates "the goodness of God in the land of the living," while it also looks forward to realities that are yet to be experienced and promises that are yet to be fulfilled. Such hope is sourced in the One who is intensely present, and yet lives beyond the present and guarantees the future.

We observed that hope is to be one of the defining marks of those who have found new life in Jesus. And what does that look like? One of the most overt indicators is **joy**. If hope is the anticipation of something wonderful, exciting and too-good-to-be-true, then such hope cannot exist apart from a sense of delight and great pleasure. Another observable evidence of hope, one that settles into the more common spaces of life, is **confidence**. Living into a larger story defined by the Author of life itself allows us to understand the seeming randomness of our experience through a different lens and to gain a perspective reserved only for those who own this hope. A third observable facet of our hope is one that adds a balancing emotion to life—**longing**. Our hope by its very nature makes us dissatisfied with all this world has to offer. We were meant to hope for more than this world can deliver.

So what practices might we deem essential to the vitality of our hope? I would suggest three that help us keep our focus on the Source of our hope and the grand narrative of His redemption.

Saturating Ourselves with The Truth

The Bible is God's personal self-disclosure. It is there that God reveals His heart and mind and ways. Our confidence in God as the source of our hope is dependent upon our knowledge of His character and the record of His faithfulness. Continually bathing our minds in the Scriptures deepens our trust in the Source of our hope.

Our hope is also based upon a complete recrafting of how we understand the story in which we find ourselves. It sources from the practice of immersing ourselves in God's Word so deeply that it not only informs our thoughts, but actually becomes, itself, a way of thinking, a way of understanding ourselves and recognizing the redemptive plot of God's story as it unfolds before us.

Praying Ourselves into The Truth

Our hope is activated by an unseen power coursing through us. The God of hope resides within us, the Holy Spirit enabling us to step out of the tyranny of a meaningless life and into the wonder of His grace. We tap into this power through prayer. I've noticed that the prayers recorded in the early letters to the churches focus on gaining a first-hand experience of spiritual realities—of our hope that is found in Jesus. Paul prays that believers would "know what is the hope of His calling," and for "the attaining of all steadfastness and patience" in light of that hope. As such prayers become our own prayers, we pray the language of hope into the fabric of our lives.

Consciously Enacting The Reality of The Truth

In addition to saturating ourselves with the Truth and praying ourselves into the Truth, we are called to be very intentional about how we step into each day and move through whatever it brings. Armed with an alternative way of thinking and an active engagement with God, we can approach life as those who are not only believing *in* something but as those who are believing *toward* something. This requires a conscious enacting of the Truth—of a hope that changes everything.

A BLESSING

Near the end of his letter to the believers in Rome, the Apostle Paul invokes a blessing of hope[32] upon them. He writes,

---

[32] Romans 15:13

"Now"
(as a present reality)
"may the God of hope"
(the One who is the source of all that we long for)
"fill you with all joy and peace"
(the practical experience of hope)
"in believing"
(the active content of our faith)
"so that you may abound with hope"
(overflowing and unconcealable)
"by the power of the Holy Spirit"
(a spiritual dynamic hidden within us)

So, as we come to the end of these conversations, may this blessing pour over you. May you "take hold of the hope set before you"[33] and "realize the full assurance of hope until the end."[34]

He is our hope!

---

[33] Hebrews 6:18
[34] Hebrews 6:11

practicing hope

epilogue

PERSONALIZING HOPE

*"that you may not grieve
as those who have no hope."*
1 Thessalonians 4:13

O n August 2, 2018, this book had been written, reviewed and edited. The text was being formatted and the cover art was being designed. Essentially, the project had been completed and it was time to celebrate what had been accomplished ... almost.

We had just returned from a couple of weeks in France, meeting with friends, exploring ancient villages and absorbing the best of French culture. We woke up to our familiar surroundings and routines—along with a moderate dose of jetlag and a flat tire on our car. While waiting for the tire to be repaired, I received a phone call from my doctor.

"Last month we removed a small lump

from your back," he began. True. A small bump had appeared on my back. My wife had spotted it and suggested I have it checked out. It had been diagnosed as a common cyst and was easily carved out by a surgeon requiring only local anesthesia and a few stitches. Done and nearly forgotten.

"We sent it out to be tested," he continued. Of course, he did. It is common practice to run a pathology on a cyst like mine. Having heard nothing from the doctor, I assumed there was nothing to talk about. I'm a healthy guy with a workout routine. Even while in France I walked an average of seven miles a day.

"I received the pathology report. I had it checked and rechecked before calling you." (Huh-oh) "The report shows that the cyst tested positive for cancer." (What?) "I'll arrange for you to meet with an oncology surgeon next week, if that's okay with you."

Finally my jetlagged brain caught up with me as I worked at absorbing the reality of what I had just heard. *Whoa!* I thought. *Let's back the truck up to that cancer part.* "Yes," I answered. "But here's the thing. I'm having a tire repaired right now and when I go home I can't just casually tell my wife, 'Oh by the way, my doctor called and says I have cancer.' She going to want more information. What else can you tell me that I can tell her?"

"I understand," he said. "You can tell her that you have a high grade pleomorphic sarcoma. Tell her that oncology surgeons recommend additional surgery as a precaution. I suggest you take your wife with you when you meet with the surgeon."

So there it was—that phone call that changes the course of your life. It only lasted three minutes. The information was matter-of-fact, clinical. But its reality was now *my* reality. And my new reality had become a case study for the hope I had just written about. What difference would this hope make in the days ahead? How would it shape my responses? How would it govern my heart?

Over the next hour I gained a cursory internet introduction to this very rare form of cancer. What I found painted a grim picture of what I might face. The five-year survival rate was not encouraging and the possible treatments sounded wretched. This sarcoma had a reputation for spreading rapidly through the body, viciously attacking vital organs. So what does hope look like now? How will the hope I possess guide how I process such information?

Ruthie and prayed together, laying it all in Jesus' hands and acknowledging that our hope is in Him and not in our circumstances. We took a deep breath and determined not to allow ourselves to be governed by what we did not yet know. The consultation was four days away—four very long days. In that pocket of time, we talked very little about the cancer and decided not to tell anyone about it until after we had met with the surgeon. Fortunately, the days were loaded with activity. We picked up our new puppy, attended a family wedding, preached in a church service and attended our granddaughter's birthday party.

Our meeting with the surgeon was brief and sobering. Any thoughts of softening the harsh realities of my diagnosis vanished as he described the cancer and patiently explained the possible scenarios. The conversation included potential therapies and life expectancy. More tests were ordered and surgery was scheduled for the last day in August.

The next six weeks were a deeply personal drama, pushing our emotions to the far edges in ways we had never experienced before. There was the surgery, an array of tests, and more consultations—each spaced just far enough apart to allow the imagination to run wild and the soul to feel the weight of possibilities.

Interestingly, I was now both the author and the reader. If the ideas developed in this book didn't make sense in this situation, if the core concepts didn't make a significant difference in my own experience, then the book should never see the light of day.

I know myself well enough to understand that I had to tether my soul to solid ground and immerse myself in a story larger than my cancer. I had choices to make that were far more important than my options for therapy. The choices I would make now would determine what story I lived into and how I would walk through these dark and threatening days.

Now it's true that this book is loaded with biblical statements addressing hope, and I could have anchored myself to any number of them. But in this time and place, I found myself gravitating to Jeremiah's poem. "These things I recall," he wrote, "and I have hope." I suppose I found common ground with the prophet because he was not hoping for some miraculous transformation of his reality. I could wish that the doctors were wrong or that God would heal me—and I did. But like Jeremiah, I had to choose where I would place my thoughts and what I would count on as the greater reality. I had to choose to believe it's true that …

> "The LORD'S lovingkindnesses
> indeed never cease,
> for His compassions never fail.
> They are new every morning.
> Great is Your faithfulness!"[35]

I found myself whispering those 3-word prayers from chapter three.

> "I adore You"
> "LORD have mercy"
> "Into Your hands"

The hope I have in Jesus has carried me through these past few months since that

---

[35] Lamentations 3:22-23

phone call on August 2nd. I have found my hope account[36] to be solvent and sustaining, far more than enough for what we have faced (or might still face). Such hope has not changed my circumstances, but it has dramatically changed my experience of those realities. This hope has been for me an anchor for the soul[37] and an overwhelming source of peace[38].

Currently, we find ourselves in a good place. The latest tests reveal no signs of cancer in my body. Although that news offers deep relief and rejoicing for the moment, the story is not over. Every six months I will need to revisit the cancer scenario again with new tests and unknown possibilities. For the next few years (or longer) I will have to live with uncertainties and choose how I will respond them. That seems to be one of the universal consistencies of life. For me, cancer demands that I consciously choose what filter I will run my thoughts through—that I choose the hope I have in Jesus … as a way of life.

---

[36] See Chapter 2
[37] See Chapter 11
[38] See Chapter 14

The Presence
discovering the God you know

At some point in our lives, many of us have the desire to become more intimate with God. The process of drawing nearer to the Creator, however, can be rife with confusion and uncertainty. In this refreshingly candid and clear study, author Steve Korch does not claim to know all the answers, but he does offer his help in demystifying the process. Formed over years of reflection and experience with this topic, these insights will provide you with tangible reference points for evaluating and building a more intimate relationship with God. "There is a craving inside each of us that longs for something more than any person or possession in this world can offer. It drives us, frustrates us and refuses to be ignored." (excerpted from *The Presence*)

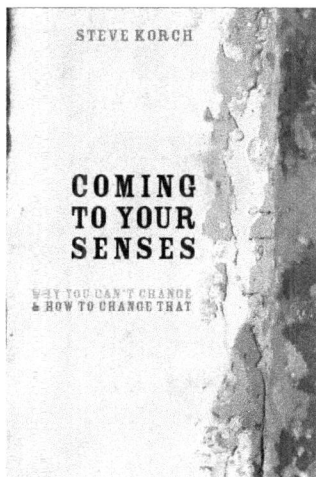

Coming to Your Senses

why you can't change
& how to change that

This book speaks to one of the most important yet least understood priorities of the Christian life ... change. Steve's passionate desire in writing this book has been to help readers discover how nurturing their spiritual senses (e.g., senses of forgiveness, identity, eternity, wonder, and presence) can lead to authentic, observable, God-honoring change.

Coming to Your Senses addresses two big questions: (1) How does God bring about authentic change in the lives of His people? (2) What does authentic change really look like?